This book is dedicated to:

Mom, Dad, Ms. Luci, Ryan, Raven, Cheyenne, Kaya, Lotus, and of course, Alaila

Multiple Sclerosis (MS) is a long-lasting illness that affects the central nervous system (brain, spinal cord, optic nerves).

People who suffer from MS have different symptoms, such as numbness, blurred vision, poor balance, trouble walking and more.

There is currently no cure for MS but, there are a lot of treatments to help cope with the symptoms, and to slow down the progression.

People with MS can live long lives, just as people without it. They just have to listen to their doctor and take good care of themselves.

Alaila's mommy calls her into the room and explains that she has Multiple Sclerosis. She learns that her mommy may need extra help at times.

Alaila notices her mommy is having a hard time walking, she helps her.

Sometimes her mommy needs a wheel chair, she is patient.

Alaila now sees her mommy is taking medicine every day.

Alaila's mommy also has a nurse that comes over to help.

Alaila's mommy is more tired than usual; she makes sure not to disturb her.

Although Alaila's mommy is not always feeling well, they still have a lot of fun together.

They travel

They go to shows.

They cook together.

They dance together.

Alaila's mommy has MS, but Alaila does not love her any less.

Author

Jessica Johnson

Instagram: @VisionsByJejo

Email: visionsbyjejo@yahoo.com

www.ingramcontent.com/pod-product-compliance
Lightning Source LLC
Chambersburg PA
CBHW041229040426
42444CB00002B/101